THE CHILDREN'S SONG BOOK

These songs are for children to sing, and for their parents to sing and play to them. Some are old, some are new, some appear in print for the first time. A few have been simplified, none has been bereft of its character, all have been lovingly treated. And as we are faithful in our ending to those songs which we loved at our beginning, may this book go with us for joy and satisfaction through all our ages.

Elizabeth Poston

BY THE SAME AUTHOR

The Baby's Song Book

Elizabeth Poston

THE CHILDREN'S
SONG BOOK

WITH DRAWINGS BY

Susan Einzig

THE BODLEY HEAD

LONDON · SYDNEY · TORONTO

Acknowledgments

I wish to thank for their help and interest in my preparation of this
book Miss Margaret Sampson and Mr Engeler of the BBC European
Service, Mr C. J. Barnard of South Africa House, Miss Liza Fuchsova,
Mr Vilem Tausky, Mme Czerwinska, Mr Francisco de Carvalho and
Mr Halvor Olsson; also Miss Doris Baker and Mr G. L. Evans of
the Hertfordshire County Library, together with my kind friends of
the BBC Central Reference and Music Libraries and of the library of
the English Folk Song and Dance Society, Cecil Sharp House. Finally,
I would like to thank especially Norman Peterkin, friend and musician,
whose lively wisdom and sympathy have been unfailing.

E.P.

ISBN 0 370 01044 2
Musical settings © Elizabeth Poston, 1961
Illustrations © The Bodley Head Ltd, 1961
Printed in Great Britain for
The Bodley Head Ltd
9 Bow Street, London WC2 E7AL
by E. Hannibal & Co Ltd, Leicester
Music engraved by Lowe & Brydone (Printers) Ltd
First published 1961
Reprinted 1967, 1971, 1979

To every child,
with one child's love
to its parents

Contents

I

The King of Spain's Daughter

I had a Little Nut Tree
Hickety, pickety, my Black Hen
Three Blind Mice
Sing a Song of Sixpence
Little Bo-peep
Baa, Baa, Black Sheep
Dog jumps through the Window
Have you seen my Love?
Ring-a-Ring o' Roses
Gira, Gira Tondo
I had Four Brothers
Aiken Drum

I had a Little Nut Tree

Traditional
arr. Elizabeth Poston

I had a little nut tree,
  Nothing would it bear
But a silver nutmeg
  And a golden pear;
The King of Spain's daughter
  Came to visit me,
And all for the sake
  Of my little nut tree.

Hickety, pickety, my Black Hen

Traditional
arr. Elizabeth Poston

At a gentle jog trot

Hick-e-ty, pick-e-ty, my black hen, She lays eggs for gen-tle-men;

Gen-tle-men come ev-'ry day To see what my black hen doth lay.

Hickety, pickety, my black hen,
She lays eggs for gentlemen;
Gentlemen come every day
To see what my black hen doth lay.

13

Three Blind Mice

Traditional
arr. Elizabeth Poston

This is fun to sing as a round, that is, with the voices chasing each other, each one after the first coming in at * and going through the song from beginning to end, round and round, till you decide to stop, when each leaves off at the last note, so that the last remaining voice or group of voices ends alone.

Three blind mice, see how they run!
They all ran after the farmer's wife,
Who cut off their tails with a carving knife,
Did ever you see such a thing in your life,
    As three blind mice?

Sing a Song of Sixpence

Traditional
arr. Elizabeth Poston

1. Sing a song of sixpence,
    A pocket full of rye;
    Four and twenty blackbirds
    Baked in a pie.
    When the pie was opened
    The birds began to sing;
    Wasn't that a dainty dish
    To set before the king?

Pitty Patty Polt

Traditional
Coll. and arr. Elizabeth Poston

Pitty patty polt,
Shoe the wild colt,
Here a nail, and there a nail,
Pitty patty polt.

You are the wild colt, and are 'shod' by taps on the sole
of your shoe, in time with the tune.

Girls and Boys come out to play

Traditional
arr. Elizabeth Poston

This come-out-to-play song to a popular country dance tune was already
a favourite with children in the time of Queen Anne.

34

Girls and boys come out to play,
The moon doth shine as bright as day.
Leave your supper and leave your sleep,
And come to your playfellows in the street.
Come with a whoop and come with a call,
Come with a good will or not at all.
Up the ladder and down the wall,
A half-penny loaf will serve us all;
You find milk, and I'll find flour,
And we'll have a pudding in half an hour.

Here we come gathering Nuts in May

Traditional
arr. Elizabeth Poston

Quick and gay

Here we come gath-er - ing nuts in May, nuts in May, nuts in May,

Here we come gath-er - ing nuts in May On a cold and frost - y morn - ing.

This is played in two lines, each line dancing up to the other. When the children have been chosen and called out by name for the two sides, they have a tug of war, and the winner gets the nuts. These probably didn't mean real nuts, but knots, meaning something twined together — posies in May. The word gave its name to the weed we call knot-grass, and to the knot gardens of formal shapes and patterns still to be seen by old houses. Purcell wrote a Knotting Song.

1. Here we come gathering nuts in May,
                    nuts in May, nuts in May,
    Here we come gathering nuts in May
    On a cold and frosty morning.

2. Who shall we have for nuts in May,
                    nuts in May, nuts in May?
    Who shall we have for nuts in May?
    On a cold and frosty morning.

3. We'll have . . . for nuts in May,
                    nuts in May, nuts in May,
    We'll have . . . for nuts in May,
    On a cold and frosty morning.

4. Who shall we send to fetch him⎫ away,
                               her ⎭
                    fetch him away, fetch him away?
    Who shall we send to fetch him away?
    On a cold and frosty morning.

5. We'll send . . . to fetch him⎫ away,
                            her ⎭
                    fetch him away, fetch him away,
    We'll send . . . to fetch him away,
    On a cold and frosty morning.

Oranges and Lemons

Traditional
arr. Elizabeth Poston

Briskly

Oran-ges and le-mons, Say the bells of St Cle-ment's. You owe me five far-things, Say the bells of St Mar-tin's. When will you pay me? Say the bells of Old Bai-ley. When I grow rich, Say the bells of Shore-ditch. When will that be? Say the bells of Step-ney. I do not know, Says the great bell of Bow Here comes a can-dle to light you to

38

bed, And here comes a chop-per to__ chop off your head.

1. Oranges and lemons,
   Say the bells of St Clement's.

2. You owe me five farthings,
   Say the bells of St Martin's.

3. When will you pay me?
   Say the bells of Old Bailey.

4. When I grow rich,
   Say the bells of Shoreditch.

5. When will that be?
   Say the bells of Stepney.

6. I do not know,
   Says the great bell of Bow.

7. Here comes a candle to light you to bed,
   And here comes a chopper to chop off your head.

A famous rhyme about the City of London's famous places,
and a game to play as you sing.

There are two churches of St Clement (St Clement's Eastcheap, and St Clement Danes) associated with the rhyme. St Martin's is thought to be St Martin's Lane in the City, not far from the Old Bailey. Shoreditch, where an old church once stood, and Stepney are outside the City walls. 'The great bell of Bow' is probably one of the peal of St Mary-le-Bow in Cheapside, which rang 'Turn again, Whittington, Lord Mayor of London.'

The game is played in a line, each child following the leader, holding on to the child in front of him, dancing along, and passing beneath an arch made by two taller players who are — secretly — one oranges, the other lemons. At the end of each verse they chant, 'Chop, chop, chop, chop' until they drop their arms round a child's head and 'chop' it. He is then asked to say in a whisper whether he chooses oranges or lemons, and takes up his place behind the one of his choice. When the game has been repeated and every child has chosen and is lined up, it ends with a tug of war between the two lines, to decide which is the stronger, oranges or lemons.

Here we go round the Mulberry Bush

Traditional
arr. Elizabeth Poston

Children dance round in a ring, stand still to perform each action,
then continue to dance round for the refrain.

40

Here we go round the mulberry bush, the mulberry bush, the mulberry bush,
Here we go round the mulberry bush
All on a frosty morning.

1. This is the way we clap our hands, this is the way we clap our hands,
This is the way we clap our hands
All on a frosty morning.

2. This is the way we stamp our feet, this is the way we stamp our feet,
This is the way we stamp our feet
All on a frosty morning.

3. This is the way we wash our face, this is the way we wash our face,
This is the way we wash our face
All on a frosty morning.

4. This is the way we brush our hair, this is the way we brush our hair,
This is the way we brush our hair
All on a frosty morning.

5. This is the way we go to bed, this is the way we go to bed,
This is the way we go to bed
All on a frosty morning.

6. This is the way we get up again, this is the way we get up again,
This is the way we get up again
All on a frosty morning.

7. This is the way we dance about, this is the way we dance about,
This is the way we dance about
All on a frosty morning.

Looby Loo

Traditional
arr. Elizabeth Poston

1. *Here we come looby loo,*
   Here we come looby light,
   Here we come looby looby,
      All on a Saturday night.

   Put your right⎱ hand in,
           left ⎰
   And put your right⎱ hand out,
              left ⎰
   Shake it a little, a little, a little,
      And turn yourself about.

      Looby, looby, looby, looby,
      Looby, looby light.

2. *Here we come, &c:*
      All on a Saturday night.

   Put your right⎱ foot in,
           left ⎰
   And put your right⎱ foot out,
              left ⎰
   Shake it a little, a little, a little,
      And turn yourself about.

      Looby, looby, looby, looby,
      Looby, looby light.

   Here we come looby loo,
   Here we come looby light,
   Here we come looby looby,
      All on a Saturday night.

A song that belongs both to England and to New England.

Sur le pont d'Avignon

French Traditional
arr. and English version
by Elizabeth Poston

Skip along to the chorus of the dance, and slow down for the actions : bow (proud and stately) for the gentlemen, curtsey (very dignified) for the ladies, salute (stiff and smart) for the soldiers, put your hands together for the monks and nuns to pray (solemn and pious), and jump about skittishly for the children — just as you might have seen these people in old days in a gay French town. There is a new bridge now over the River Rhône at Avignon — the old one, said to have been built centuries ago by a shepherd-boy saint, is in ruins, but children still sing its rhyme.

44

Sur le pont d'Avignon,
L'on y danse, l'on y danse,
Sur le pont d'Avignon,
L'on y danse tout en rond.

On the bridge, on the bridge,
See them dancing, see them dancing,
On the bridge, on the bridge,
On the bridge at Avignon.

1. Les beaux messieurs font comm' ci,
   Et puis encore comm' ça.

   Sur le pont, &c.

1. The gentlemen bow this way,
   Then again bow that way.

   On the bridge, &c.

2. Les belles dames font comm' ci,
   Et puis encore comm' ça.

   Sur le pont, &c.

2. The ladies curtsey this way,
   Then they curtsey that way.

   On the bridge, &c.

3. Les soldats font comm' ci,
   Et puis encore comm' ça.

   Sur le pont, &c.

3. The soldiers salute this way,
   Then they salute that way.

   On the bridge, &c.

4. Les capucines font comm' ci,
   Et puis encore comm' ça.

   Sur le pont, &c.

4. The monks and nuns pray this way,
   Then again pray that way.

   On the bridge, &c.

5. Les gamins font comm' ci,
   Et puis encore comm' ça.

   Sur le pont, &c.

5. The children all play this way,
   And again play that way.

   On the bridge, &c.

Skip to my Lou

American Traditional
arr. Elizabeth Poston

Rather quick, light

Skip, skip, skip to my Lou, Skip, skip, skip to my Lou,

Skip, skip, skip to my Lou, Skip to my Lou, my dar - ling.

This singing game comes from America. Form two circles, one inside the other, boys on the inside, partners facing one another. For the first verse, all skip round. At 'Partner's gone, what will I do?' the girls on the outside stand still, while the boys continue to skip round. At the refrain 'Skip to my Lou, my darling' each boy takes a new partner, and the game goes on again.

Skip, skip, skip to my Lou,
Skip, skip, skip to my Lou,
Skip, skip, skip to my Lou,
 Skip to my Lou, my darling.

Partner's gone, what will I do?
Partner's gone, what will I do?
Partner's gone, what will I do?
 Skip to my Lou, my darling.

Skip, skip, &c.

The Paw-paw Patch

American Traditional
arr. Elizabeth Poston

Rather quick, at the right speed for dancing

Where, oh where is pret-ty lit-tle Su - sie?

Where, oh where is pret-ty lit-tle Su - sie? Where, oh where is

pret-ty lit-tle Su - sie? 'Way down yon-der in the paw - paw patch.

The paw-paw is a fruit that grows in the southern U.S.A., where this song comes from. You dance it in two lines of couples, boys one side, girls the other. Verse 1, the girl in the first couple at the head of the line skips round to the right, goes round both lines and skips back to her place. Verse 2, the same girl repeats this pattern, but this time the boys follow, then skip back to their places. Verse 3, the couples join hands, and following the first couple, again skip round to the right. When the top couple reach the bottom of the line, they make an arch through which the other couples dance back to their places. The second couple now becomes the first, and the game continues. Each verse may be sung twice if once through isn't long enough.

1. Where, oh where is pretty little Susie?
   Where, oh where is pretty little Susie?
   Where, oh where is pretty little Susie?
   'Way down yonder in the paw-paw patch.

2. Come on, boys, let's go find her,
   Come on, boys, let's go find her,
   Come on, boys, let's go find her,
   'Way down yonder in the paw-paw patch.

3. Come on, boys, bring her back again,
   Come on, boys, bring her back again,
   Come on, boys, bring her back again,
   'Way down yonder in the paw-paw patch.

This Way, that-a Way

American Traditional
arr. Elizabeth Poston

When I was a lit-tle boy, lit-tle ol' lit-tle boy,
Dad-dy came and got me, came and got me,

When I was a lit-tle boy five years old,
Dad-dy did-n't scold me, I've been told.

CHORUS

Ha - ha! this-a way,

Ha - ha! that-a way, Ha - ha! this-a way, Then, oh then.

This is a going-back-to-school song from the southern U.S.A. Sing it with a strong
beat; at ' Ha-ha ! this-a way ' bend to the left; at ' Ha-ha ! that-a way ' bend to the
right, and at ' Then, oh then ' clap your hands.

1. When I was a little boy, little ol' little boy,
    When I was a little boy five years old,
    Daddy came and got me, came and got me,
    Daddy didn't scold me, I've been told.

    Ha-ha! this-a way,
    Ha-ha! that-a way,
    Ha-ha! this-a way,
        Then, oh then.

2. I went into school there, little ol' school there,
    Went into the school there, school so old;
    Learned the Golden Rule there, little ol' rule there,
    Learned the Golden Rule there, I've been told.

    Ha-ha! &c.

3. Learned my lesson, little ol' lesson,
    Learned my lesson like I was told.
    Wasn't that a blessing, little ol' blessing?
    Learned my lesson at five years old.

    Ha-ha! &c.

4. Met my teacher, little ol' teacher,
    Met my teacher, he didn't scold;
    Said ' I'm glad ter meetcha, meetcha, meetcha,'
    Said ' I'm glad ter meetcha,' I've been told.

    Ha-ha! &c.

May Day in the Morning

Traditional
arr. Elizabeth Poston

In polka time, with spirit

There was a crane sat on a stone, He flew a-way and there was none; An-

oth-er came and there was one, 'Twas May Day in the morn - ing.

An American version of a Scottish rhyme.

1. There was a crane sat on a stone,
   He flew away and there was none;
   Another came and there was one,
      'Twas May Day in the morning.

2. There was a cat skinned up a tree
   To see whatever was to see,
   When he fell down, then down fell he,
      'Twas May Day in the morning.

3. There was a rooster in a trough
   Who got a touch of whooping-cough,
   He sneezed his tail and feathers off,
      'Twas May Day in the morning.

4. There was a farmer made a wish
   That he could swim like any fish,
   They popped him in the chafing dish,
      'Twas May Day in the morning.

Over the Hills and Far Away

Traditional
arr. Elizabeth Poston

Quick and gay

Tom he_ was a_ pip-er's son, He learnt to_ play when he was young, And

all_ the tune that he could play Was 'Ov-er the hills and far a-way'.

Ov-er the hills and a great way off, The wind shall blow my_ top-knot off.

This tune was so popular in England over 200 years ago,
that John Gay put it into *The Beggar's Opera*.

1. Tom he was a piper's son,
   He learnt to play when he was young,
   And all the tune that he could play
   Was ' Over the hills and far away'.
   Over the hills and a great way off,
   The wind shall blow my top-knot off.

2. Tom with his pipe made such a noise,
   That he pleased both girls and boys,
   And they stopped to hear him play
   ' Over the hills and far away'.
   Over the hills and, &c.

III

The Apple Tree

The Apple Tree

Words collected by Joshua Smith
in New Hampshire, 1784

Music by
Elizabeth Poston

This beauty doth all things excel,
By faith I know, but ne'er can tell
The glory which I now can see
In Jesus Christ the apple tree.

This may also be sung unaccompanied as a round, voices entering at *

58

Morning Hymn

Words adapted from a prayer of
St Richard of Chichester, 1197-1253

Music by
Elizabeth Poston

In moderate time, freely

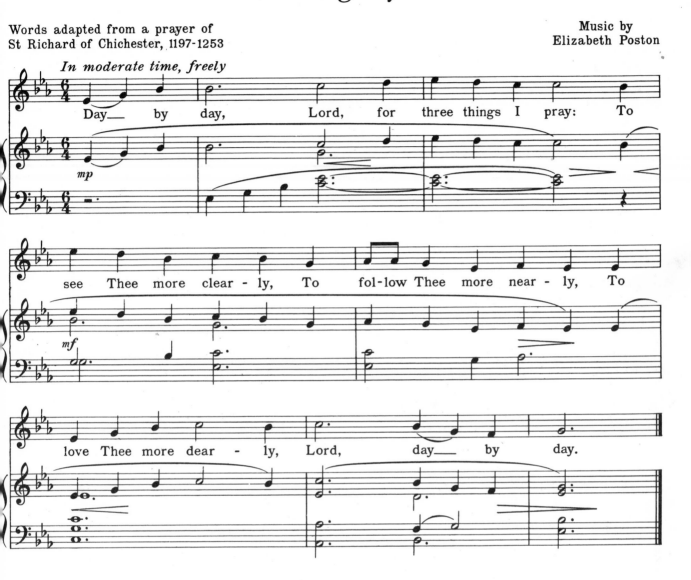

Day— by day, Lord, for three things I pray: To see Thee more clear - ly, To fol-low Thee more near - ly, To love Thee more dear - ly, Lord, day— by day.

Day by day, Lord, for three things I pray:

To see Thee more clearly,

To follow Thee more nearly,

To love Thee more dearly.

Saint Richard of Chichester preached a crusade against the Saracens.
He showed pity to animals, and died at Dover in 1253.

Evening Hymn.   Tallis's Canon

Words by
Bishop Ken, 1637-1711

Music by
Thomas Tallis, c. 1510-1585

Rather slow, with dignity

Glo - ry to thee, my God, this night For all the bless-ings of the light; Keep

me, O keep me, King of Kings, Be - neath thy own al - might - y wings.

To sing unaccompanied as a round, in canon, use the first two lines above, voices
joining in to enter at *.

1. Glory to thee, my God, this night
   For all the blessings of the light;
   Keep me, O keep me, King of Kings,
   Beneath thy own almighty wings.

2. Forgive me, Lord, for thy dear Son,
   The ill that I this day have done,
   That with the world, myself, and thee,
   I, ere I sleep, at peace may be.

3. Teach me to live, that I may dread
   The grave as little as my bed;
   Teach me to die, that so I may
   Rise glorious at the aweful day.

4. O may my soul on thee repose,
   And with sweet sleep mine eyelids close,
   Sleep that may me more vigorous make
   To serve my God when I awake.

5. Praise God, from whom all blessings flow;
   Praise him, all creatures here below;
   Praise him above, ye heavenly host;
   Praise Father, Son, and Holy Ghost.

The Lamb

Words by
William Blake, 1757-1827

Music by
Elizabeth Poston

With simplicity

Lit - tle Lamb, who made thee? Dost thou know who made thee? Gave thee life, and
Lit - tle Lamb, I'll tell thee, Lit - tle Lamb, I'll tell thee: He is call - ed

bid thee feed By the stream and o'er the mead; Gave thee cloth-ing of de-light,
by thy name, For he calls him-self a Lamb, He is meek, and he is mild;

Soft-est cloth-ing, wool-ly, bright; Gave thee such a ten-der voice, Mak-ing all the
He be-came a lit-tle child. I a child, and thou a lamb, We are call-ed

vales re-joice? Lit-tle Lamb, who made thee? Dost thou know who made thee?
by his name. Lit-tle Lamb, God bless thee! Lit - tle Lamb, God   bless thee!

Little Lamb, who made thee?
Dost thou know who made thee?
Gave thee life, and bid thee feed
By the stream and o'er the mead;
Gave thee clothing of delight,
Softest clothing, woolly, bright;
Gave thee such a tender voice,
Making all the vales rejoice?
Little Lamb, who made thee?
Dost thou know who made thee?

Little Lamb, I'll tell thee,
Little Lamb, I'll tell thee:
He is called by thy name,
For he calls himself a Lamb,
He is meek, and he is mild;
He became a little child.
I a child, and thou a lamb,
We are called by his name.
Little Lamb, God bless thee!
Little Lamb, God bless thee!

Loving Shepherd of Thy Sheep

Words by
Jane Leeson, 1807-1882

Tune by John Wesley, 1703-1791
harm. Elizabeth Poston

At a moderate, flowing speed

Lov - ing Shep-herd of_ thy sheep, Keep thy_ lamb, in safe - ty keep;

No - thing can thy_ power with-stand, None can pluck me_ from thy hand.

1. Loving Shepherd of thy sheep,
   Keep thy lamb, in safety keep;
   Nothing can thy power withstand,
   None can pluck me from thy hand.

2. I would bless thee every day,
   Gladly all thy will obey,
   Like the blessèd ones above,
   Happy in thy precious love.

3. Loving Shepherd, ever near,
   Teach thy lamb thy voice to hear;
   Suffer not my steps to stray
   From the straight and narrow way.

4. Where thou leadest I would go,
   Walking in thy steps below,
   Till before my Father's throne
   I shall know as I am known.

His Jewels

Words by
the Rev. W. O. Cushing

Tune by G. F. Root
arr. Elizabeth Poston

With a gentle lilt

When he com - eth, when he com - eth To make up his

jew - els, All his jew - els, pre-cious jew - els, His loved and his own;

CHORUS

Like the stars of the morn - ing, His__ bright crown a - dorn - ing, They shall

shine in their beau - ty, Bright gems for his crown.

1. When he cometh, when he cometh
   To make up his jewels,
   All his jewels, precious jewels,
   His loved and his own;

   > *Like the stars of the morning,*
   > *His bright crown adorning,*
   > *They shall shine in their beauty,*
   > *Bright gems for his crown.*

2. He will gather, he will gather
   The gems for his kingdom;
   All the pure ones, all the bright ones,
   His loved and his own.

   > *Like the stars &c.*

3. Little children, little children,
   Who love their Redeemer,
   Are the jewels, precious jewels,
   His loved and his own.

   > *Like the stars &c.*

67

Spring Carol

Tune Traditional *O Filii et Filiae,*
arr. Elizabeth Poston

Words anonymous

Broad, with a strong swing

REFRAIN

Al - le - lu - ia,— Al - le - lu - ia, Al - le - lu - ia! The Spring, the Spring a - gain— is here, The gen - tle leaves and flow'rs ap - pear, And Eas - ter Day— with joy— draws near: Al - le - lu - ia!

The tune of this early dance-carol is probably French.

Alleluia, Alleluia, Alleluia!

1. The Spring, the Spring again is here,
    The gentle leaves and flowers appear,
    And Easter Day with joy draws near:
            Alleluia!

Alleluia, Alleluia, Alleluia!

2. The earth new-born, lifts up her voice,
    The sun and moon and stars rejoice,
    The birds now tune their merry noise:
            Alleluia!

Alleluia, Alleluia, Alleluia!

3. Let hill and vale and all around
    Re-echo to the happy sound,
    All creatures' voices now are found:
            Alleluia!

Carol of the Annunciation
(Angelus ad Virginem)

Words and Tune early 14th cent.,
arr. and English version
by Elizabeth Poston

Gა - bri-el to Ma - ry came, A gen - tle mes - sage bare he;
Deep in awe the Maid - en bowed, To hear him say_ 'Hail Ma - ry'.

There, heaven and earth re-ceived his call, 'Hail, hail thou queen of vir - gins

all; Thou, yet un-de-filed, Shalt bear a child Of sov'reign grace, To com-fort all_ man-

kind; Thou shalt bear him, Lord and God of all, To save our sin - ful race.'

70

1. Gabriel to Mary came,
   A gentle message bare he;
Deep in awe the Maiden bowed,
   To hear him say 'Hail, Mary.'
There, heaven and earth received his call,
'Hail, hail thou queen of virgins all;
   Thou, yet undefiled,
   Shalt bear a child
   Of sovereign grace,
To comfort all mankind;
   Thou shalt bear him,
   Lord and God of all,
   To save our sinful race.'

2. 'How shall this befall,' quoth she,
   'To me, a virgin lowly?
How can I deny the vows
   That bind me to be holy?'
Then said the Angel, 'Maid, believe
God's Holy Ghost shall this achieve,
   So be not afraid,
   But now rejoice,
   Rejoice indeed
For ever in his sight;
   For thy trust shall be
   In his mercy,
   By God's especial might.'

3. Then bespoke the Maid again,
   Within her lowly bower,
'I the humble handmaid am
   Of God's almighty power.
So to his messenger most blest,
Bearing in secret his behest,
   I will answer
   And obey with love
   And holy joy
The tidings I have heard;
   For I bow before
   Thy holy will,
   According to thy word.'

4. Maid, and Mother of us all,
   Who bore the gift God gave us,
Praise we now in earth and heav'n
   Thy Son who came to save us.
Pray thou thy child, the Lord of love,
That he may hear in heav'n above,
   And may succour
   And redeem us
   By his holy birth,
And save us when we roam;
   That by his good grace
   We may find place
   In heaven's eternal home.

The earliest carols were sung and danced, and this one tells
the story with a tune in dance movement.

71

Once in Royal David's City

Words by
Mrs C. F. Alexander, 1818-1895

Music by
H. J. Gauntlett 1805-1875

In moderate time

Once in roy - al Da - vid's ci - ty Stood a low - ly cat - tle_ shed,
Where a moth - er laid_ her_ ba - by In a man - ger for_ a _ bed:

Ma - ry was that moth-er mild, Je - sus Christ her lit - tle_ child.

1. Once in royal David's city
    Stood a lowly cattle shed,
   Where a mother laid her baby
    In a manger for his bed:
   Mary was that mother mild,
   Jesus Christ her little child.

2. He came down to earth from heaven,
    Who is God and Lord of all,
   And his shelter was a stable,
    And his cradle was a stall:
   With the poor, and mean, and lowly,
   Lived on earth our Saviour holy.

3. And through all his wondrous childhood
       He would honour and obey,
    Love and watch the lowly maiden,
       In whose gentle arms he lay:
    Christian children all must be
    Mild, obedient, good as he.

4. For he is our childhood's pattern:
       Day by day like us he grew,
    He was little, weak, and helpless,
       Tears and smiles like us he knew;
    And he feeleth for our sadness,
    And he shareth in our gladness.

5. And our eyes at last shall see him,
       Through his own redeeming love,
    For that child so dear and gentle
       Is our Lord in heaven above;
    And he leads his children on
    To the place where he is gone.

6. Not in that poor lowly stable,
       With the oxen standing by,
    We shall see him; but in heaven,
       Set at God's right hand on high;
    When like stars his children crowned
    All in white shall stand around.

St Joseph's Carol

Traditional Flemish
arr. and English version
by Elizabeth Poston

O see a young maid - moth - er ly - ing, Full of
Hear what gift to her_ is giv - en, 'Tis a

grace and great - ly blest; Je - sus, Child of Na - za -
son, by God's be - hest.

reth Be - fore_ us bit - ter - ly lies cry - ing, Hush, O

hush, thou lit - tle babe, hush, God has willed thou li - est here thus.

1. O see a young maid-mother lying,
   Full of grace and greatly blest;
   Hear what gift to her is given,
   'Tis a son, by God's behest.
   Jesus, Child of Nazareth
   Before us bitterly lies crying,
       Hush, O hush, thou little babe, hush,
       God has willed thou liest here thus.

2. St Joseph near, in awe beholding,
   Reverently holds hat in hand,
   By the blessed Virgin Mother
   There, so thoughtful, he doth stand.
   In the world around him wending,
   Sees he folk of grief unending,
       Hush, O hush, thou little babe, hush,
       God has willed thou liest here thus.

3. St Joseph he set forth a-trudging
   Barefoot through the winter snow;
   Wood and coal he must be seeking,
   And 'tis well that he does so;
   For, unwrapped, unwarmed, the Babe,
   Behold him, as his mother holds him,
       Hush, O hush, thou little babe, hush,
       God has willed thou liest here thus.

This is a Flemish folk carol from Belgium, which gives a picture of St Joseph as the peasants imagined him — like one of the figures you see in the snowy landscapes of the Flemish masters. One of the special things about Christmas carols is that they are continually seen afresh in the minds of peoples of many races and climates, and so the carols are like the countries they come from.

This carol is included here by permission of Messrs Schott Frères, Brussels.

The Holy Family

Italian folk rhyme
collected, arr. and English version
by Elizabeth Poston

With a gentle lilt

Ma - ry washed lin - en, Jo - seph spread it dry - ing, The
Ba - by was sleep - y And sore - ly was cry - ing. 'O
hush you, my ba - by, For now I will tend you, I'll take you and I'll rock you, And
sing lul - la - by, I'll take you and I'll rock you, And sing_ lul - la - by.'

This is a picture of the Holy Family, leading their life at home like any other family —
such as you may see in the great Italian paintings. The country people in Italy spread
their washing to dry on the ground, and on walls and bushes.

1. Mary washed linen,
   Joseph spread it drying,
   The Baby was sleepy,
   And sorely was crying.

2. 'O hush you, my baby,
   For now I will tend you,
   I'll take you and I'll rock you,
   And sing lullaby.'

All-the-Year Carol
Tomorrow shall be my Dancing Day

Traditional
arr. Elizabeth Poston

Rather fast, with an easy lilt (1 in a bar stress)

To-mor-row shall be__ my danc-ing day: I would my true__ love did__ so chance To__ see the le-gend of__ my play, To call my true love to__ my dance. Sing O, my love, O__ my love, my love, my love; This have I done__ for my__ true love.

Love and the dance that are of God and man are in this dance carol and its words,
which are probably a version of much older ones.

1. Tomorrow shall be my dancing day:
      I would my true love did so chance
   To see the legend of my play,
      To call my true love to my dance:

   Sing O my love, O my love, my love, my love;
      This have I done for my true love.

2. Then was I born of a virgin pure,
      Of her I took fleshly substance;
   Thus was I knit to man's nature,
      To call my true love to my dance:

   Sing O my love, &c.

3. In a manger laid and wrapped I was,
      So very poor, this was my chance,
   Betwixt an ox and a silly poor ass,
      To call my true love to my dance:

   Sing O my love, &c.

4. Then afterwards baptized I was,
      The Holy Ghost on me did glance,
   My Father's voice heard from above,
      To call my true love to my dance:

   Sing O my love, &c.

(Lent : Passiontide)

5. Into the desert I was led,
      Where I fasted without substance:
   The devil bade me make stones my bread,
      To have me break my true love's dance:

   Sing O my love, &c.

6. The Jews on me they made great suit,
      And with me made great variance,
   Because they loved darkness rather than light,
      To call my true love to my dance:

   Sing O my love, &c.

7. For thirty pence Judas me sold,
      His covetousness for to advance;
   'Mark whom I kiss, the same do hold,'
      The same is he shall lead the dance:

   Sing O my love, &c.

(Passiontide : Easter : Ascension)

8. Before Pilate the Jews me brought,
      Where Barabbas had deliverance;
   They scourged me and set me at nought,
      Judged me to die to lead the dance:

   Sing O my love, &c.

9. Then on the cross hangèd I was,
      Where a spear to my heart did glance;
   There issued forth both water and blood,
      To call my true love to my dance:

   Sing O my love, &c.

10. Then down to hell I took my way
       For my true love's deliverance,
    And rose again on the third day,
       Up to my true love and the dance:

    Sing O my love, &c.

11. Then up to heaven I did ascend,
       Where now I dwell in sure substance,
    On the right hand of God, that man
       May come unto the general dance:

    Sing O my love, &c.

IV
My Mind to me a Kingdom is

My Mind to me a Kingdom is

Words by
Leonard Clark

Music by
Elizabeth Poston

At a moderate speed, happily

My mind to me a king-dom is; I have a world in-side me Of peace-ful ways and shin-ing days, And saints who walk be-side me.

My mind to me a kingdom is;
I have a world inside me
Of peaceful ways and shining days,
And saints who walk beside me.

My world is full of heaven's joy,
No evils cloud its pleasure,
I gladly bless my happiness,
Love is my greatest treasure.

A sixteenth-century poet of the time of the first Queen Elizabeth wrote a poem beginning
' My mind to me a kingdom is '. Now, in our own time, a poet of the second Queen
Elizabeth has written a new poem on the old poet's first line.

Matthew, Mark, Luke and John

Words Traditional

Music by
Elizabeth Poston

Peacefully

Mat-thew, Mark, Luke and John, Bless the bed_that I lie on,

Finis

Mat-thew, Mark, Luke and John, Bless the bed_that I lie on.

Four cor-ners to my bed, Four an-gels round my head:

meno p

D.C.

One to watch, and one to pray, And two to bear my soul a-way.

poco cresc.

84

Matthew, Mark, Luke and John,
Bless the bed that I lie on.
  Four corners to my bed,
  Four angels round my head:
  One to watch and one to pray
  And two to bear my soul away.

The Gentle Shepherd

Words by
Edward Moore, 1756

Music anonymous
arr. Elizabeth Poston

Tell me, lovely Shepherd, where
Thou feed'st at noon thy fleecy care?
Direct me to the sweet retreat
That guards thee from the mid-day heat,
Lest by the flocks I lonely stray
Without a guide, and lose my way.
Where rest at noon thy bleating care?
Lovely Shepherd, tell me where?

The Three Ravens

Traditional
arr. Elizabeth Poston

1. There were three ravens sat on a tree,
    Down a down, hey down, hey down,
   There were three ravens sat on a tree,
    With a down;
   There were three ravens sat on a tree,
   They were as black as they might be.
    With a down, derry, derry, derry, down, down.

2. The one of them said to his mate,
   ' Where shall we our breakfast take? '

3. ' Down in yonder green field,
   There lies a knight slain under his shield.

4. ' His hounds they lie down at his feet,
   So well they can their master keep.

5. ' His hawks they fly so eagerly,
   There's no fowl dare him come nigh.'

6. Down there comes a fallow doe,
   As great with young as she might go.

7. She lift up his bloody head,
   And kissed his wounds that were so red.

8. She got him up upon her back,
   And carried him to earthen lake.

9. She buried him before the prime,[1]
   She was dead herself ere evensong time.

10. God send every gentleman
    Such hawks, such hounds, and such a leman.[2]

A ballad common to Scotland and England, full of the magic of legend.

[1] *prime*, the first of the appointed hours of the Church, i.e., 6 a.m.
[2] *leman*, sweetheart.

The Little Horses

American folk lullaby
arr. Elizabeth Poston

Quiet and sleepy

Hush you bye, Don' you cry,

Go to sleep-y, lit-tle ba - by; When you wake, You shall have cake, An'

drive those pret-ty lit-tle hor - ses. hor - ses.

1. Hush you bye,

    Don' you cry,

    Go to sleepy, little baby;

    When you wake,

    You shall have cake,

    An' drive those pretty little horses.

2. Hush you bye,

    Don' you cry,

    Go to sleepy, little baby;

    Blacks and bays,

    Dapples and grays,

    An' coach and six-a little horses.

In America the coloured people are fond of singing to the plucked string accompaniment
of banjo or guitar. This gives the song a deep lilt, and that is why the piano part here
is made in the same way.

Since first I saw your Face

Words anonymous

Music by
Thomas Ford, 1607

Since first I saw your face I re-solved To hon - our and re - nown ye. If now I be dis - dained I__ wish My heart had nev - er known__ ye. What, I that loved and you that liked Shall we be-gin to wran - gle? No, no, no, no, no, my heart is fast, And can - not dis - en - tan - gle.

Thomas Ford was a court musician and lutenist who was born in the reign of Queen Elizabeth I and died in the reign of King Charles I. This love song comes from his *Musicke of Sundry Kindes*.

The piano part has been adapted from the transcription by Dr. E. H. Fellowes in *The English Lutenists*, by courtesy of Messrs. Stainer and Bell, Ltd.

1. Since first I saw your face I resolved
       To honour and renown ye.
   If now I be disdained I wish
       My heart had never known ye.
   What, I that loved and you that liked
       Shall we begin to wrangle?
   No, no, no, my heart is fast,
       And cannot disentangle.

2. The sun whose beams most glorious are
       Rejecteth no beholder;
   And your sweet beauty past compare
       Made my poor eyes the bolder.
   Where Beauty moves and Wit delights
       And signs of kindness bind me,
   There, O there, where'er I go,
       I'll leave my heart behind me.

Robin loves me

Adam de la Hale, 1285
accompaniment by Elizabeth Poston

In moderate time

Rob - in___ loves me, I am his; Rob - in sought me

For his___ true love, He'll have me. Rob - in___ bought me

Pret - ty fav - ours, Scar - let___ fav - ours Fine and bon - ny,

Gown and gir - dle All for my plea-sure, All for my___ own.

This is an early song called a Rondel. Adam de la Hale, who wrote it, was a French
poet and musician, and it was sung by Marion in his play *The Pleasant Pastime of
Robin and Marion.*

1. Robin loves me,
    I am his ;
    Robin sought me
    For his true love,
    He'll have me.

2. Robin bought me
    Pretty favours,
    Scarlet favours,
    Fine and bonny,
    Gown and girdle
    All for my pleasure,
    All for my own.

95

Lullaby

Traditional Manx lullaby tune
arr. Elizabeth Poston

O— hush thee my dove, O hush thee my row-an, O— hush thee my lap-wing, my lit-tle brown bird; O— fold thy wing and seek thy nest now, O— shine the ber-ry— on the bright tree; The bird is— home from the moun-tain and val-ley, O— hush thee my bird-ie, my pret-ty dear-ie.

O hush thee my dove, O hush thee my rowan,
O hush thee my lapwing, my little brown bird;
O fold thy wing and seek thy nest now,
O shine the berry on the bright tree;
The bird is home from the mountain and valley,
O hush thee my birdie, my pretty dearie.

Greensleeves

Traditional
arr. Elizabeth Poston

This song, which Shakespeare knew (Sir John Falstaff and Mistress Ford refer to it in *The Merry Wives of Windsor*) has kept its popularity for some 400 years. The tune has had many different words in all sorts of versions: it has been used as a carol, a political ballad, a dance and piece for the lute and virginals, and for hangings at Tyburn. Pepys wrote of it in his diary, John Gay put it into *The Beggar's Opera*, and Vaughan Williams used it in *Sir John in Love*.

1. Alas! my love, you do me wrong
      To cast me off discourteously,
    And I have lovèd you so long,
      Delighting in your company.
        Greensleeves was all my joy,
        Greensleeves was my delight,
        Greensleeves was my heart of gold,
        And who but my lady Greensleeves.

2. I bought thee petticoats of the best,
      The cloth so fine as might be;
    I gave thee jewels for thy chest,
      And all this cost I spent on thee.
        Greensleeves was &c.

3. Thy smock of silk, both fair and white,
      With gold embroidered gargeously;
    Thy petticoat of sendal[1] right,
      And these I bought thee gladly.
        Greensleeves was &c.

4. My gayest gelding I thee gave
      To ride whenever likèd thee,
    No lady ever was so brave,
      And yet thou would'st not love me.
        Greensleeves was &c.

5. Well will I pray to God on high
      That thou my constancy may'st see,
    And yet that once before I die
      Thou wilt vouchsafe to love me.
        Greensleeves farewell, adieu!
        God I pray to prosper thee,
        For I am still thy lover true,
        Come once again and love me.

[1] *sendal*, thin silk

Have you seen but a White Lily grow

Anonymous, 16th century
arr. Elizabeth Poston

Rather slow

Have you seen but a white li-ly grow___ Be-fore rude hands have touch'd it? Have you mark'd but the fall of the snow Be-fore the earth hath smutch'd it? Have you felt the wool of bea-ver, Or swan's down___ ev-er? Or have smelt of the bud of the bri-er, Or the nard in the fire? Or have tast-ed the bag of the bee? O so

white,   O so soft,   O so sweet, so sweet,__ so sweet is she.   O so   she.

Have you seen but a white lily grow

Before rude hands have touch'd it?

Have you mark'd but the fall of the snow

Before the earth hath smutch'd it?

Have you felt the wool of beaver,

Or swan's down ever?

Or have smelt of the bud of the brier,

Or the nard[1] in the fire?

Or have tasted the bag of the bee?

O so white, O so soft,

O so sweet, so sweet is she.

[1]*nard*, a sweet-smelling balsam

Fairest Isle

Words by
John Dryden, 1631-1700

Music by Henry Purcell, 1659-1695
edited by Elizabeth Poston

In moderate time, with graceful movement

Fair-est Isle, all isles___ ex-cell - ing, Seat___ of Plea - sures
Ve - nus here will choose___ her dwell - ing, And___ for-sake___ her

and___ of Loves;
Cyp - rian groves.
Cu - pid from his fav - 'rite na - tion,

Care___ and En - vy will___ re - move; Jea-lous - y that

poi - sons Pas - sion, And___ Des-pair___ that dies___ for Love.

A song in honour of England in Purcell's opera *King Arthur*,
in which it is sung by Venus, the goddess of love.

Fairest Isle, all isles excelling,
  Seat of Pleasures and of Loves;
Venus here will choose her dwelling,
  And forsake her Cyprian groves.

Cupid from his fav'rite nation
  Care and Envy will remove;
Jealousy that poisons Passion,
  And Despair that dies for Love.

Gentle murmurs, sweet complaining,
  Sighs that blow the fire of Love;
Soft repulses, kind disdaining
  Shall be all the pains you prove.

Ev'ry swain shall pay his duty,
  Grateful ev'ry Nymph shall prove;
And as these excel in beauty,
  Those shall be renown'd for Love.

It was a Lover and his Lass

Words by
William Shakespeare, 1564-1616

Music by
Thomas Morley, 1557-c.1603

Quick and light

It was a lov-er and his lass, With a hey, and a ho, and a hey____ no-ni-

no, and a hey____ no-ni no-ni - no, That o'er the green corn-field did pass, In

spring time, in spring time, in spring time, The on-ly pret-ty ring time, When

birds do sing, Hey ding a ding a ding, hey ding a ding a ding, hey

ding a ding a ding, Sweet lov-ers love the spring. In spring time, in spring

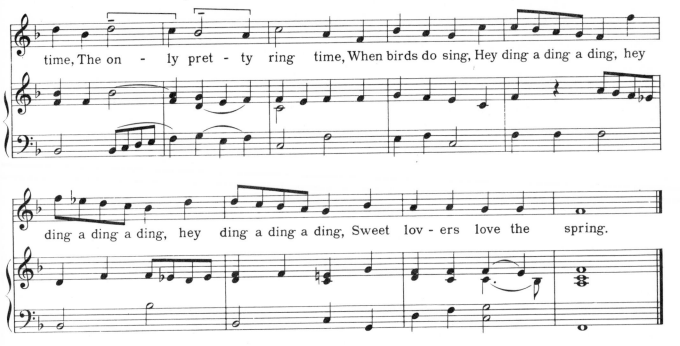

time, The on - ly pret - ty ring time, When birds do sing, Hey ding a ding a ding, hey

ding a ding a ding, hey ding a ding a ding, Sweet lov - ers love the spring.

1. It was a lover and his lass,

    With a hey, and a ho, and a hey nonino,

    That o'er the green cornfield did pass,

    In spring time,

    The only pretty ring time,

    When birds do sing,

    Hey ding a ding, ding,

    Sweet lovers love the spring.

2. Between the acres of the rye,

    With a hey, and a ho, and a hey nonino,

    These pretty country folks would lie,

    In spring time, &c.

3. This carol they began that hour,

    With a hey, and a ho, and a hey nonino,

    How that life was but a flower,

    In spring time, &c.

4. And therefore take the present time,

    With a hey, and a ho, and a hey nonino,

    For love is crownéd with the prime,

    In spring time, &c.

The song sung by the two Pages to Touchstone, the clown, in the Forest of Arden, in Shakespeare's comedy *As You Like It.* The tune is of Shakespeare's own time, and comes from Thomas Morley's *Little Short Songs.* The piano part has been simplified from the transcription by Dr E. H. Fellowes in *The English Madrigalists* by courtesy of Messrs Stainer and Bell, Ltd.

V

Where the Bee Sucks

Where the Bee sucks

Words by
William Shakespeare, 1564-1616

Air by Robert Johnson, died *c*.1634
arr. Elizabeth Poston

Happy, rather lively

Where the bee sucks there suck I, ___ In a cow-slip's bell I lie, There I couch when owls do cry, On the bat's back I do fly Af - ter sum-mer mer - ri - ly.

[Keeping the same pulse]

Mer - ri - ly, mer - ri - ly, shall I live now, Un - der the blos-som that hangs on the bough, Mer - ri - ly, mer - ri - ly, shall I live now,

Un - der the blos - som that hangs on the bough.

The song sung by the spirit Ariel in Shakespeare's play *The Tempest*, after his master, the magician Prospero, has promised to set him free. The composer of the music was a court musician who lived in Shakespeare's time.

Where the bee sucks there suck I,
In a cowslip's bell I lie,
There I couch when owls do cry,
On a bat's back I do fly
    After summer merrily.
Merrily, merrily, shall I live now,
Under the blossom that hangs on the bough.

Summer is i-cumen in

13th century

With a marked, springy lilt

Sum - mer is i-cum - en in,___ Loud - e sing cuc - koo;

Grow - eth seed and blow - eth mead And spring th the wood a - new.

Sing cuc - koo! Ewe___ bleat - eth af - ter lamb, Loweth

af - ter calf the cow; Bul - lock start - eth, buck he vert - eth;

Mer - rie sing cuc-koo. Cuc - koo, cuc - koo,___ Well singst thou, cuc-

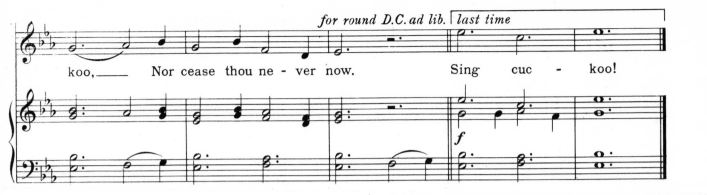

Summer is i-cumen in,

Loudë[1] sing cuckoo ;

Groweth seed and bloweth mead

And springth the wood anew.

Sing cuckoo !

Ewe bleateth after lamb,

Loweth after calf the cow ;[1]

Bullock starteth, buck he verteth ;

Merrie sing cuckoo.

Cuckoo, cuckoo,

Well singst thou, cuckoo,

Nor cease thou never now.[1]

[1] Pronounce loudë as loodë, cow as coo, and now as noo to get the best ryhme.

One of the earliest English songs to come down to us, a rota or round from the West Country, and still loved to-day. * Marks the entry of voices after the first. Two lower voices (here placed in the left hand of the piano part) sing a burden repeating 'Sing cuckoo'.

Now is the Month of Maying

Thomas Morley, 1557–c.1603

Fast and light

Now is the month of may - ing, When mer - ry lads are play - ing Fa la

la la la la la la la, Fa la la la la la la. Now la. Each

with his bon - ny lass Up - on the green - y grass. Fa la

la la la, fa la la la la la la, Fa la la la la. Each la.

An Elizabethan dance song called a Ballet. Barley-break was a favourite open-air
game (a sort of 'Tom Tiddler's Ground') played by couples in the stack-yard. Two
English poets, Sir Philip Sidney and Robert Herrick, have written about it.

1. Now is the month of maying,
    When merry lads are playing
        Fa la la la la la la la la,
        Fa la la la la la la la.
    Each with his bonny lass
    Upon the greeny grass.
        Fa la la la la,
        Fa la la la la la la,
        Fa la la la la.

2. The Spring, clad all in gladness,
    Doth laugh at Winter's sadness,
        Fa la, &c.
    And to the bagpipe's sound
    The nymphs tread out their ground.
        Fa la, &c.

3. Fie then! why sit ye musing,
    Youth's sweet delight refusing?
        Fa la, &c.
    Say, dainty nymphs, and speak,
    Shall we play barley-break?
        Fa la, &c.

When Daisies Pied

Words by
William Shakespeare, 1564–1616

Music by
Thomas Arne, 1710–1778

Moderately fast, gracefully

When dais - ies pied, and vi - o - lets blue, And la - dy-smocks all

sil - ver white; And cuc-koo buds of yel - low hue Do paint the mead-ows

with de-light: The cuc-koo then on ev - 'ry tree, Mocks mar-ried men, mocks mar-ried men,

Mocks mar-ried men; for thus sings he, Cuc-koo. Cuc-koo, Cuc-koo, Cuc-koo, Cuc-koo:

O word of fear, O word of fear, Un-

pleas-ing to a mar-ried ear, Un-pleas-ing to_ a mar-ried ear!_____

When daisies pied, and violets blue,
 And lady-smocks all silver white;
And cuckoo buds of yellow hue
 Do paint the meadows with delight:
The cuckoo then on every tree,
Mocks married men; for thus sings he,
   Cuckoo.
Cuckoo, Cuckoo: O word of fear,
Unpleasing to a married ear!

When shepherds pipe on oaten straws,
 And merry larks are ploughmen's clocks:
When turtles[1] tread, and rooks and daws,
 And maidens bleach their summer smocks:
The cuckoo then on every tree,
Mocks married men; for thus sings he,
   Cuckoo.
Cuckoo, Cuckoo: O word of fear,
Unpleasing to a married ear!

[1] turtle doves

Cowboy Spring

American Cowboy song
arr. Elizabeth Poston

At a happy jog-trot

It is spring, the dais - ies are bust - ing out, It is spring, the grass is ten - der, And the breeze is blow - ing so soft - ly O - ver the rol - ling plains.

A spring song of the Cowboys of the Western States. 'Double-X' is a mark used in branding cattle.

116

1. It is spring, the daisies are busting out,
   It is spring, the grass is tender,
   And the breeze is blowing so softly
   Over the rolling plains.

2. Me and my horse go clippety cloppety,
   Me and my horse go jiggety, joggety,
   As we go riding clippety, cloppety
   Over the rolling plains.

3. I just left the Double-X Ranch,
   I got on my horse and rode away,
   I know a pretty girl lives in the valley,
   Over the rolling plains.

Lavender's Blue

Traditional
arr. Elizabeth Poston

1. Lavender's blue, diddle, diddle,
    Lavender's green;
   When I am king, diddle, diddle,
    You shall be queen.

2. Call up your men, diddle, diddle,
    Set them to work,
   Some to the plough, diddle, diddle,
    Some to the cart.

3. Some to make hay, diddle, diddle,
    Some to cut corn,
   While you and I, diddle, diddle,
    Keep ourselves warm.

The Angler's Song

Words by
John Chalkhill, *fl.* 1600

Tune by Henry Lawes, 1596-1662
arr. Elizabeth Poston

Happy and vigorous

Man's life is but vain, For 'tis sub-ject to pain, And sor-row, and short as a bub-ble; 'Tis a hodge-podge of busi-ness, And mo-ney and care, And care and mo-ney and trou-ble.

Three 17th century contemporaries come together in this song, which Izaak Walton liked so much that he put it into *The Compleat Angler*, his famous book on fishing.

1. Man's life is but vain,
        For 'tis subject to pain,
        And sorrow, and short as a bubble;
      'Tis a hodge-podge of business,
        And money and care,
        And care and money and trouble.

2. But we'll take no care
        When the weather proves fair,
        Nor will we vex now though it rain;
      We will banish all sorrow,
        And sing till tomorrow,
        And angle and angle again.

Harvest Home

Words as traditionally sung,
based on John Dryden, 1631-1700

Traditional
arr. Elizabeth Poston

You can hear the stamp of heavy boots in this country song that should be sung with a very rousing chorus. Harvest Home in England was traditionally celebrated with feasting and merry-making on the farms. The lines about the parson refer to the payment to him of tithes (a tenth of the land produce of the parish), and to the complaint that he kept his flock waiting for their Sunday dinner by preaching too long a sermon!

122

1. Our oats they are hoed, and our barley's reap'd,
    Our hay it is mow'd, and our hovels heap'd.

    Come, boys, come! Come, boys, come!
    And merrily roar out Harvest Home!
    Harvest Home! Harvest Home!
    We'll merrily roar out Harvest Home!

2. We've cheated the parson, we'll cheat him again;
    For why should the Vicar have one in ten?

    One in ten, one in ten,
    For why should the Vicar have one in ten?
    One in ten, one in ten,
    For why should the Vicar have one in ten?

3. For staying while dinner is cold and hot,
    And pudding and dumpling are burnt to pot?

    Burnt to pot, burnt to pot,
    And pudding and dumpling are burnt to pot.
    Burnt to pot, burnt to pot,
    And pudding and dumpling are burnt to pot.

4. We'll toss off our ale till we can't stand,
    And hey! for the honour of Old England!

    Old England! Old England!
    And hey! for the honour of Old England!
    Old England, Old England!
    And hey! for the honour of Old England!

The North Wind doth Blow

Traditional
arr. Elizabeth Poston

The north wind doth blow,
And we shall have snow,
And what will poor robin do then?
    Poor thing.
He'll sit in a barn
To keep himself warm,
And hide his head under his wing,
    Poor thing.

124

Pastime with Good Company

King Henry VIII, *reigned* 1509-1547
Edited and arr. Elizabeth Poston

Brisk and vigorous

Pas - time with good com - pa - ny I love, and shall un-

til ___ I die; Grudge who will, but none ___ de - ny, So

God be pleas'd __ this life ___ will I: For my pas - tance, Hunt,

sing and dance; My heart ___ is set. All good - ly

sport To my com - fort, Who shall __ me ___ let?

1. Pastime with good company
    I love, and shall until I die;
    Grudge who will, but none deny,
    So God be pleas'd this life will I:
       For my pastance,[1]
       Hunt, sing and dance;
       My heart is set.
         All goodly sport
         To my comfort,
       Who shall me let?[2]

2. Youth will needs have dalliance[3]
    Of good or ill some pastance;
    Company me thinketh the best
    All thoughts and fancies to digest.
       For idleness
       Is chief mistress
       Of vices all:
         Then who can say
         But pass the day
       Is best of all?

3. Company with honesty
    Is virtue,—and vice to flee:
    Company is good or ill,
    But ev'ry man hath his free will.
       The best I sue,
       The worst eschew:[4]
       My mind shall be
         Virtue to use:
         Vice to refuse
       Thus shall I use me.

[1]*pastance*, pastime   [2]*let*, hinder
[3]*have dalliance*, to amuse oneself, to make love   [4]*eschew*, avoid

This song is preserved in the King's Manuscript in the British Museum. Its common-sense and strong, vigorous tune are characteristic of the royal author, and in spite of its high moral tone, it gives us a good picture of King Henry's pastimes: his love of hunting, music, dance and dalliance — all, in fact, that he chose to embrace as 'goodly sport.'

I saw Three Ships

Traditional
arr. Elizabeth Poston

1. I saw three ships come sailing by,
        Sailing by, sailing by,
    I saw three ships come sailing by
        On New Year's Day in the morning.

2. And what do you think was in them then,
        In them then, in them then,
    And what do you think was in them then,
        On New Year's Day in the morning.

3. Three pretty girls were in them then,
        In them then, in them then
    Three pretty girls were in them then,
        On New Year's Day in the morning.

4. And one could whistle, and one could sing,
        One could sing, one could sing,
    And one could play on the violin
        On New Year's Day in the morning.

5. Such joy there was at my wedding,
        My wedding, my wedding,
    Such joy there was at my wedding,
        On New Year's Day in the morning.

Wassail Song

Traditional
arr. Elizabeth Poston

Here we come a-was-sail-ing a-mong the leaves of green; —

Here we come a-wan-der-ing, so fair-ly to be seen. —

CHORUS

Our jol-ly was-sail, our jol-ly was-sail, Love and joy come to

you, and to our was-sail bough; Pray God bless you, and send you a

hap-py New Year, a New Year, a New Year, Pray God

bless you, and send you a hap - py New Year. ___

1. Here we come a-wassailing among the leaves of green;

    Here we come a-wandering so fairly to be seen.

    Our jolly wassail, our jolly wassail,

    Love and joy come to you, and to our wassail bough;

    Pray God bless you, and send you a happy New Year.

2. We are not daily beggars, that beg from door to door,

    We are the neighbour's children, whom you have seen before.

    Our jolly wassail, &c.

3. I have a little purse, it is made of leather skin,

    I want a little sixpence, to line it well within.

    Our jolly wassail, &c.

4. Bring us out the table, and spread it with the cloth;

    Bring us out the bread and cheese, and a bit of your Christmas loaf.

    Our jolly wassail, &c.

5. God bless the master of this house, and the mistress too;

    And the little children, which round the table grew.

    Our jolly wassail, &c.

The word wassail was the traditional way of saying 'Good health', and Christmas wassailing was one of the happiest English customs. This wassail song comes from Yorkshire, where the children used to go round singing it from door to door, carrying green boughs, and asking for a New Year's gift.

VI

I See You

I see you

Jag ser dig

Swedish children's singing game
arr. and English version
by Elizabeth Poston

To play this game, form couples, boys in front, each girl holding the shoulders of the boy in front of her, the couples facing one another. For the first half of the song, the girl peeks over the boy's snoulder, first right, then left, in time with the music. For the second half of the song, the girls skip round to the right of their partners, take hands and skip round in a circle, till the last line of the words ' Then you take me and I take you,' when each girl takes her partner's hands and they skip round together, finishing with the girls in front. The game then begins again.

134

© Elizabeth Poston 1961

I see you, I see you,
   Tra la la la la la.
I see you, I see you,
   Tra la la la la la.
You see me and I see you,
Then you take me and I take you,
You see me and I see you,
Then you take me and I take you.

Kookaburra

Australian rhyme
arr. Elizabeth Poston

Quick and jaunty

Koo - ka - bur - ra sits on an old gum tree, ____

Mer - ry lit - tle King of the Bush is he. ____ Laugh, Koo - ka - bur - ra,

laugh, Koo - ka - bur - ra, Gay your life must be.

The Kookaburra or laughing kingfisher is an Australian bird who gets his name from his call. This song also makes a good round.

Kookaburra sits on an old gum tree,
Merry little King of the Bush is he.
Laugh, Kookaburra, laugh, Kookaburra,
Gay your life must be.

My Old Top

Mon Vieux Moine

French Canadian folk song
arr. and English version
by Elizabeth Poston

Rather quick, lively

If my old top were a danc - ing man, A hood I'd give him to keep him warm! Top, you keep on turn - ing, As bright my fire is burn - ing; But you don't hear my mill wheels' song, And you don't hear how my mill runs on.

138

1. If my old top were a dancing man,
       A hood I'd give him to keep him warm!
          Top, you keep on turning,
          As bright my fire is burning;
          But you don't hear my mill wheels' song,
          And you don't hear how my mill runs on.

2. If my old top were a dancing man,
       A sash to wear I would give him then!
          Top, you keep, &c.

Aunt Hessie's White Horse

Tant Hessie se Witperd

South African folk song
arr. and English version
by Elizabeth Poston

Can't you see Aunt Hes-sie's white horse, Aunt Hes-sie's white horse, Aunt Hes-sie's white horse, Oh can't you see Aunt Hes-sie's white horse, And gee-up a trot for me? Don't you call him slow, Aunt Hes-sie will make him go; He'll gal-lop a-long so fine, He'll make the whole world mine. Oh __

Aunt Hessie's white horse is a rocking horse.

Can't you see Aunt Hessie's white horse,
    Aunt Hessie's white horse, Aunt Hessie's white horse,
Oh can't you see Aunt Hessie's white horse,
    And gee-up a trot for me?
        Don't you call him slow,
        Aunt Hessie will make him go;
        He'll gallop along so fine,
        He'll make the whole world mine. Oh—
Can't you see, &c.

Cotton Field

Jamaican folk song
arr. Elizabeth Poston

Quick and jazzy

I pick up my hoe an' I go, I
pick up my hoe an' I go - o - o, Come wid me an' help hoe a
row, An' we'll hoe an' we'll hoe an' we'll hoe.

1. I pick up my hoe an' I go,
    I pick up my hoe an' I go-o-o,
    Come wid me an' help hoe a row,
    An' we'll hoe an' we'll hoe an' we'll hoe.

2. I hoe where de young cotton grow,
    I hoe where de young cotton grow-ow-ow,
    O help hoe a young cotton row,
    An' we'll hoe an' we'll hoe an' we'll hoe.

Lovely Rosa

Schöne Rosa

German folk song
arr. and English version
by Elizabeth Poston

Rather slow

All se - cret - ly the moon comes up, Blue, blue,

blos-som blue; The sil-ver clouds her sil-ver cup, Blue, blue, blos-som blue.

Blos-som in flow'r, Maid - en in bow'r, O love-ly Ro - sa!

A minstrel's song, which a much later German composer, Brahms, liked so much that
he put it into the slow movement of one of his piano sonatas.

144

All secretly the moon comes up,
  Blue, blue, blossom blue;
The silver clouds her silver cup,
  Blue, blue, blossom blue.
    Blossom in flow'r,
    Maiden in bow'r,
O lovely Rosa!

Stork Long-o'-Leg

Stork lange Bein

Danish Traditional
arr. and English version
by Elizabeth Poston

Stork, stork, long-o'-leg, Tell me where you've been, I beg;

Say, did you see the Great Py-ra-mid, Far in the land of King Phar-aoh?

In Denmark the red-legged storks — who stand on one leg, and also live far away
in Africa — nest on the roof-tops.

1. Stork, stork, long-o'-leg,
   Tell me where you've been, I beg;
   Say, did you see the Great Pyramid,
   Far in the land of King Pharaoh?

2. Stork, stork, long-o'-leg,
   Standing in your stockings red,
   Say, did you leave your other leg
   Far in the land of King Pharaoh?

3. Stork, stork, long-o'-leg,
   Happy blessings on your head;
   Say, have you brought little gifts for us
   Under your wing, for to share, O?

4. Stork, stork, long-o'-leg,
   Tell us now your news, we beg;
   Say, are you holding above our bed,
   Brother or sister so fair, O?

Father

Tatíček

Czech Traditional
arr. and English version
by Elizabeth Poston

Father, O Father dear, Be with your chil-dren here; In our home, in ev-'ry wea-ther, Hap-py times we'll have to-geth-er, Hap-py while you are near.

Father, O Father dear,
Be with your children here;
   In our home, in ev'ry weather,
   Happy times we'll have together,
Happy while you are near.

The Little Bird

Lata Ptaszek po ulicy

Polish children's singing game
arr. and English version
by Elizabeth Poston

Little bird - ie, hop - ping gai - ly, In the street I

see you dai - ly,
Hop - ping here and hop - ping there, —
Hop - ping here and hop - ping there, —

Peck - ing crumbs to take your nest;
You're the one I like the best. —

This is the Polish version of Ring o' Roses. The child in the ring is the little bird
hopping about, while the other children skip round him, until at the last line he chooses
one, who then takes his place instead in the centre of the circle. What makes it especially
Polish is the tune, which is a Mazurka, one of Poland's national dances.

Little birdie, hopping gaily,
In the street I see you daily,
Hopping here and hopping there,
Pecking crumbs to take your nest;
Hopping here and hopping there,
You're the one I like the best.

I'm the King of the Castle

Il mio bel castello

Italian children's singing game
arr. and English version
by Elizabeth Poston

In steady time

mf

I'm the King of the Cas-tle, Ti - ro, ti - ro, ti - ro, tel -

lo, I'm the King of the Cas - tle. Ti - ro, ti - ro, ti - ro

la. We have come to rob your cas-tle, Ti - ro, ti - ro, ti - ro, tel -

lo, We have come to rob your cas-tle. Ti - ro, ti - ro, ti - ro la.

This is played in two lines, the robbers and the defenders marching up to each other
alternately, till they break loose and all mix up together at the end.

1. I'm the King of the Castle,
   Tiro, tiro, tiro, tello,
   I'm the King of the Castle.
   Tiro, tiro, tiro la.

2. We have come to rob your castle,
   Tiro, tiro, &c.

3. We'll defend our castle,
   Tiro, tiro, &c.

4. We'll set fire to your castle,
   Tiro, tiro, &c.

5. We will put it out again,
   Tiro, tiro, &c.

6. We will fire all our cannon,
   Tiro, tiro, &c.

I've a Fine Bonny Castle

Yo tengo un castillo

**Spanish children's singing game
arr. and English version
by Elizabeth Poston**

Gay

poco f

I've a fine, bon-ny cas-tle, Ma-ta ril-lay ril-lay ril-lay, I've a fine, bon-ny cas-tle. Ma-ta ril-lay ril-lay ril-lay ron.

This is the Spanish version of the castle game, sung in two lines, dancing up to each
other and back. At the end all join hands.

1. I've a fine, bonny castle,
       Mata rillay rillay rillay,
    I've a fine, bonny castle.
       Mata rillay rillay ron.

2. May I come to your castle?
       Mata rillay, &c.

3. Yes, do come to my castle.
       Mata rillay, &c.

4. But you've locked up your castle.
       Mata rillay, &c.

5. Find the key of my castle.
       Mata rillay, &c.

6. Where's the key of your castle?
       Mata rillay, &c.

7. The key's in the sea.
       Mata rillay, &c.

8. Let me search till I find it.
       Mata rillay, &c.

9. You must swim to the bottom.
       Mata rillay, &c.

10. Here's the key of your castle.
       Mata rillay, &c.

11. Then we'll all go together,
       Mata rillay rillay rillay,
    And we'll play in the garden.
       Mata rillay rillay ron.

Pico Serenico

Portuguese Traditional
arr. and English version
by Elizabeth Poston

Come a - long, O come a - long, my lit-tle ho — ney, Put your

foot a-long o' mine and come and dance; Now I'm read-y, now I'm read-y, O my

dear one, O come on and join the dance. Pi-co, pi-co se-re-ni - co,

With a gay bal-loon for hide-and-seek - O, Pick-a pick-a - po-sy for your

sweet - heart On the feast of our good Saint John. Come a-

1. Come along, O come along, my little honey,
    Put your foot along o' mine and come and dance;
    Now I'm ready, now I'm ready, O my dear one,
    O come on and join the dance.
        Pico, pico serenico,
        With a gay balloon for hide-and-seek-O,
        Pick-a pick-a-posy for your sweetheart
        On the feast of our good Saint John.

    Come along, O come along, my little honey,
    Let us join our hands and dance along tonight;
    Hop-a-skip-a, hop-a-skip-a all together,
    As you tell me your heart's delight.
        Pico, pico serenico,
        Laugh as you dance the Tirolico,
        Peek-a peek-a playing hide-and-seek-O,
        On the feast of our good Saint John.

In the month of June the feast of Saint John is celebrated in Portugal with dancing in
the streets with coloured balloons all night until daybreak. 'Pico serenico' is a sort
of 'pat-a-cake' game, played by picking out the fingers on your hand in time with
the words.

Index of First Lines

Index of Titles